SCHIRMER PERFORMANCE EDITIONS

HAL LEONARD PIANO LIBRARY

BEETHOVEN
PIANO SONATA NO. 11
IN B-FLAT MAJOR
Op. 22

T0082006

Edited and Recorded by Robert Taub

Also Available:
BEETHOVEN PIANO SONATAS
edited and recorded by Robert Taub

Volume I, Nos. 1–15
00296632 Book only
00296634 CDs only (5 disc set)

Volume II, Nos. 16–32
00296633 Book only
00296635 CDs only (5 disc set)

On the cover:
The Tree of Crows, 1822 (oil on canvas)
by Caspar David Friedrich
(1774–1840)
© Louvre, Paris, France/Giraudon/The Bridgeman Art Library

ISBN 978-1-4768-1623-4

G. SCHIRMER, Inc.

DISTRIBUTED BY

7777 W. BLUEMOUND RD. P.O. BOX 13819 MILWAUKEE, WI 53213

www.schirmer.com
www.halleonard.com

CONTENTS

PAGE	TRACK	
4		BEETHOVEN AND THE PIANO SONATAS
6		PERFORMANCE NOTES
		Piano Sonata No. 11 in B-flat Major, Opus 22
9	1	Allegro con brio
18	2	Adagio con molta espressione
22	3	Menuetto
24	4	Rondo: Allegretto
32		ABOUT THE EDITOR

BEETHOVEN
AND THE PIANO SONATAS

In 1816, Beethoven wrote to his friend and admirer Carl Czerny: "You must forgive a composer who would rather hear his work just as he had written it, however beautifully you played it otherwise." Having lost patience with Czerny's excessive interpolations in the piano part of a performance of Beethoven's *Quintet for Piano and Winds*, Op. 16, Beethoven also addressed the envelope sarcastically to "Herr von Zerni, celebrated virtuoso." On all levels, Beethoven meant what he wrote.

As a composer who bridged the gulf between court and private patronage on one hand (the world of Bach, Handel, Haydn, and Mozart) and on the other hand earning a living based substantially on sales of printed works and/or public performances (the world of Brahms), Beethoven was one of the first composers to become almost obsessively concerned with the accuracy of his published scores. He often bemoaned the seeming unending streams of mistakes. "Fehler—fehler!—Sie sind selbst ein einziger Fehler" ("Mistakes—mistakes!—You yourselves are a unique mistake") he wrote to the august publishing firm of Breitkopf und Härtel in 1811.

It is not surprising, therefore, that toward the end of his life Beethoven twice (1822 and again in 1825) begged his publishers C.F. Peters and Schott to bring out a comprehensive complete edition of his works over which Beethoven himself would have editorial control, and would thus be able to ensure accuracy in all dimensions—notes, pedaling and fingering, expressive notations (dynamics, slurs), and articulations, and even movement headings. This never happened.

Beethoven was also obsessive about his musical sketches that he kept with him throughout his mature life. Desk sketchbooks, pocket sketchbooks: thousands of pages reveal his innermost compositional musings, his labored processes of

creativity, the ideas that he abandoned, and the many others—often jumbled together—that he crafted through dint of extraordinary determination, single-minded purpose, and the inspiration of genius into works that endure all exigencies of time and place. In the autograph scores that Beethoven then sent on to publishers, further layers of the creative processes abound. But even these scores might not be the final word in a particular work; there are instances in which Beethoven made textual changes, additions, or deletions by way of letters to publishers, corrections to proofs, and/or post-publication changes to first editions.

We can appreciate the unique qualities of the Beethoven piano sonatas on many different levels. Beethoven's own relationship with these works was fundamentally different from his relationship to his works of other genres. The early sonatas served as vehicles for the young Beethoven as both composer and pianist forging his path in Vienna, the musical capital of Europe at that time. Throughout his compositional lifetime, even when he no longer performed publicly as a pianist, Beethoven used his thirty-two piano sonatas as crucibles for all manner of musical ideas, many of which he later re-crafted—often in a distilled or more rarefied manner—in the sixteen string quartets and the nine symphonies.

The pianoforte was evolving at an enormous rate during the last years of the eighteenth century extending through the first several decades of the nineteenth. As a leading pianist and musical figure of his day, Beethoven was in the vanguard of this technological development. He was not content to confine his often explosive playing to the smaller sonorous capabilities of the instruments he had on hand; similarly, his compositions demanded more from the pianofortes of the day—greater depth of sonority, more subtle levels of keyboard finesse and control, and increased registral range.

These sonatas themselves pushed forward further development and technical innovation from the piano manufacturers.

Motivating many of the sonatas are elements of extraordinary—even revolutionary—musical experimentation extending into domains of form, harmonic development, use of the instrument, and demands placed upon the performer, the piano, and the audience. However, the evolution of these works is not a simple straight line.

I believe that the usual chronological groupings of "early," "middle," and "late" are too superficial for Beethoven's piano sonatas. Since he composed more piano sonatas than substantial works of any other single genre (except songs) and the period of composition of the piano sonatas extends virtually throughout Beethoven's entire creative life, I prefer chronological groupings derived from more specific biographical and stylistic considerations. I delve into greater depth on this and other aspects of the sonatas in my book *Playing the Beethoven Piano Sonatas* (Amadeus Press).

1795–1800: Sonatas Op. 2 no. 1, Op. 2 no. 2, Op. 2 no. 3, Op. 7, Op. 10 no. 1, Op. 10 no. 2, Op. 10 no. 3, Op. 13, Op. 14 no. 1, Op. 14 no. 2, Op. 22, Op. 49 no. 1, Op. 49 no. 2

1800–1802: Sonatas Op. 26, Op. 27 no. 1, Op. 27 no. 2, Op. 28, Op. 31 no. 1, Op. 31 no. 2, Op. 31 no. 3

1804: Sonatas Op. 53, Op. 54, Op. 57

1809: Sonatas Op. 78, Op. 79, Op. 81a

1816–1822: Sonatas Op. 90, Op. 101, Op. 106, Op. 109, Op. 110, Op. 111

From 1804 (post-Heiligenstadt) forward, there were no more multiple sonata opus numbers; each work was assigned its own opus. Beethoven no longer played in public, and his relationship with the sonatas changed subtly.

—*Robert Taub*

PERFORMANCE NOTES

Extracted from *Beethoven: Piano Sonatas Volume I*, edited by Robert Taub.

For the preparation of this edition, I have consulted autograph scores, first editions, and sketchbooks whenever possible. (Complete autograph scores of only twelve of the piano sonatas—plus the autograph of only the first movement of Sonata Op. 81a—have survived.) I have also read Beethoven's letters with particular attention to his many remarks concerning performances of his day and the lists of specific changes/corrections that he sent to publishers. We all know—as did Beethoven—that musical notation is imperfect, but it is the closest representation we have to the artistic ideal of a composer. We strive to represent that ideal as thoroughly and accurately as possible.

Tempo

My recordings of these sonatas are available as companions to the two published volumes. I have also included my suggestions for tempo (metronome markings) for each sonata, at the beginning of each movement.

Fingering

I have included Beethoven's own fingering suggestions. His fingerings—intended not only for himself (in earlier sonatas) but primarily for successive generations of pianists—often reveal intensely musical intentions in their shaping of musical contour and molding of the hands to create specific musical textures. I have added my own fingering suggestions, all of which are aimed at creating meaningful musical constructs. As a general guide, I believe in minimizing hand motions as much as possible, and therefore many of my fingering suggestions are based on the pianist's hands proceeding in a straight line as long as musically viable and physically practicable. I also believe that the pianist can develop senses of tactile feeling for specific musical patterns.

Pedaling

I have also included Beethoven's pedal markings in this edition. These indications are integral parts of the musical fabric. However, since most often no pedal indication is offered, whenever necessary one should use the right pedal—sparingly and subtly—to help achieve legato playing as well as to enhance sonorities.

Ornamentation

My suggestions regarding ornamental turns concern the notion of keeping the contour smooth while providing an expressive musical gesture with an increased sense of forward direction. The actual starting note of a turn depends on the specific context: if it is preceded by the same note (as in Sonata Op. 10 no. 2, second movement, m. 42), then I would suggest that the turn is four notes, starting on the upper neighbor: upper neighbor, main note, lower neighbor, main note.

Sonata in F Major, Opus 10 no. 2:
second movement, m. 42, r.h.

However, if the turn is preceded by another note (as in Sonata Op. 10 no. 2, first movement, m. 38), then the turn could be five notes in total, starting on the main note: main note, upper neighbor, main note, lower neighbor, main note.

Sonata in F Major, Opus 10 no. 2:
first movement, m. 38, r.h.

Whenever Beethoven included an afterbeat (Nachschlag) for a trill, I have included it as well. When he did not, I have not added any.

Footnotes

Footnotes within the musical score offer contextual explanations and alternatives based on earlier representations of the music (first editions, autograph scores) that Beethoven had seen and corrected. In areas where specific markings are visible only in the autograph score, I explain the reasons and context for my choices of musical representation. Other footnotes are intended to clarify ways of playing specific ornaments.

Notes on the Sonata[1]

PIANO SONATA NO. 11 IN B-FLAT MAJOR, OPUS 22 (1800)

Sonata Op. 22, a wonderful piece, is played less frequently than many, perhaps because the gentle last movement does not excite audiences to a fevered pitch.

The **Allegro con brio** of Op. 22 is full of life, with a high level of enthusiasm that seems to bubble just barely beneath the surface. I prefer a quick, spirited tempo, and make the opening measures very light, with the right-hand sixteenth notes well articulated. This approach propels the listener forward to the main line beginning in m. 4, which is the only true melody of the entire exposition. When the left hand has the theme in mm. 11–12, curved fingers and clear articulation will help counteract any impulse to rush. I consider the *sforzandos* in mm. 16, 18, and 20 to be sharp impulses within a general context of *piano*, with a further drop to *pianissimo* for the start of the second theme. Although the dominant is reached as early as m. 38, which could mark the end of the exposition, further embellishments and repeated arrivals on the dominant continue for another thirty measures. Leading up to each of these dominant arrivals, I like to give the impression by preparing the cadence that the section is coming to an end, but then play through the surprising continuations maintaining a trajectory all the way to m. 68.

In the development, I drop from repeated levels of *fortissimo* to levels of *piano* when elements of the first theme return in different keys (mm. 83, 87, and 91). In m. 105, in ever lower registers, the left hand plays the line that closed the exposition until reaching the lowest note on Beethoven's piano (low F, m. 116). I hold the fermata in m. 127 long enough to preserve the inherent tension of the *pianissimo* dominant chord, but not so long that the sound dies away completely.

From the outset, the **Adagio con molta espressione** is full of operatic lyricism. I play the opening left-hand chords with a pure accompaniment touch—flat fingers gently sweeping off the keys. In the canon that follows the surprising move to G major in m. 31, I like to establish terraces of voices, keeping each one independent in dynamics from the others. To create the illusion of a crescendo on the sustained top and bottom B-flats in both mm. 43 and 44, I make a slight swell with the inner voices but then allow them to drop again as the last two eighth notes of the top and bottom voices continue the crescendo. When the main theme returns in m. 47, I allow the embellished areas to be relaxed in pacing, in the nature of a true singing, breathing line. At the end of the movement, I wait before the penultimate chord to make sure that the last two chords will indeed be very soft.

In the beginning of the **Menuetto**, I make a distinct difference between the singing top line and the accompaniment. This difference blurs in mm. 9 and 13, though, where I make the hands more equal, possibly even favoring the left hand the second time through. I also play the initial eight-bar phrase differently in its first and second appearances: the first time arises out of silence and is softer. Keeping a steady tempo in the overtly dramatic Minore trio will allow the offbeat *sforzando* right-hand chords to sound more menacing than a pacing that rushes.

I have found that the most successful performances of the **Rondo: Allegretto** are those that do not try to make this movement into something it isn't, but rather accept the music for what it is— gentle and graceful—and revel in it. The tempo is not fast; it is leisurely. Even when octaves enter in the right hand in m. 9, they are not virtuosic, but rather simply a fuller, more open, singing line. Throughout, harmonies are firmly grounded.

In the coda, I make sure to keep an eighth-note pulse within the seemingly long quarter notes with which it starts (mm. 182–183) in order not to rush. The left-hand fingers are firm and articulate the thirty-second notes smoothly.

1 Excerpted from *Playing the Beethoven Piano Sonatas* by Robert Taub
edited and abridged by Susanne Sheston
© 2002 by Robert Taub
Published by Amadeus Press
Used by permission.

PIANO SONATA NO. 11 IN B-FLAT MAJOR, Opus 22

Dedicated to Countess von Browne

Sonata in B-flat Major

Ludwig van Beethoven
Opus 22
Composed in 1800

Allegro con brio (♩ = 132)

11.

a) Many editions print this chord as D–F (see m. 174); however, both the first edition (Hoffmeister & Kühnel, Leipzig) and the copy revised by Beethoven show a G instead of F.

b) C also in the revised copy, not B-flat as in some editions.

c) correct here as G–B-flat; see footnote to m. 43

Adagio con molta espressione ($♪$ = 96)

d) short appoggiatura e) The turn can be played on the second sixteenth of the second eighth. f) Play the turn before the sixteenth-note B-flat.

MENUETTO (♩ = 108)

Menuetto da capo senza replica

RONDO
Allegretto (♪ = 126)

g) [music example] h) Play the turn before the dotted-sixteenth-note C.

i) This bar is configured differently from m. 33 because the range of Beethoven's piano at this time did not extend above f³. j) without tail

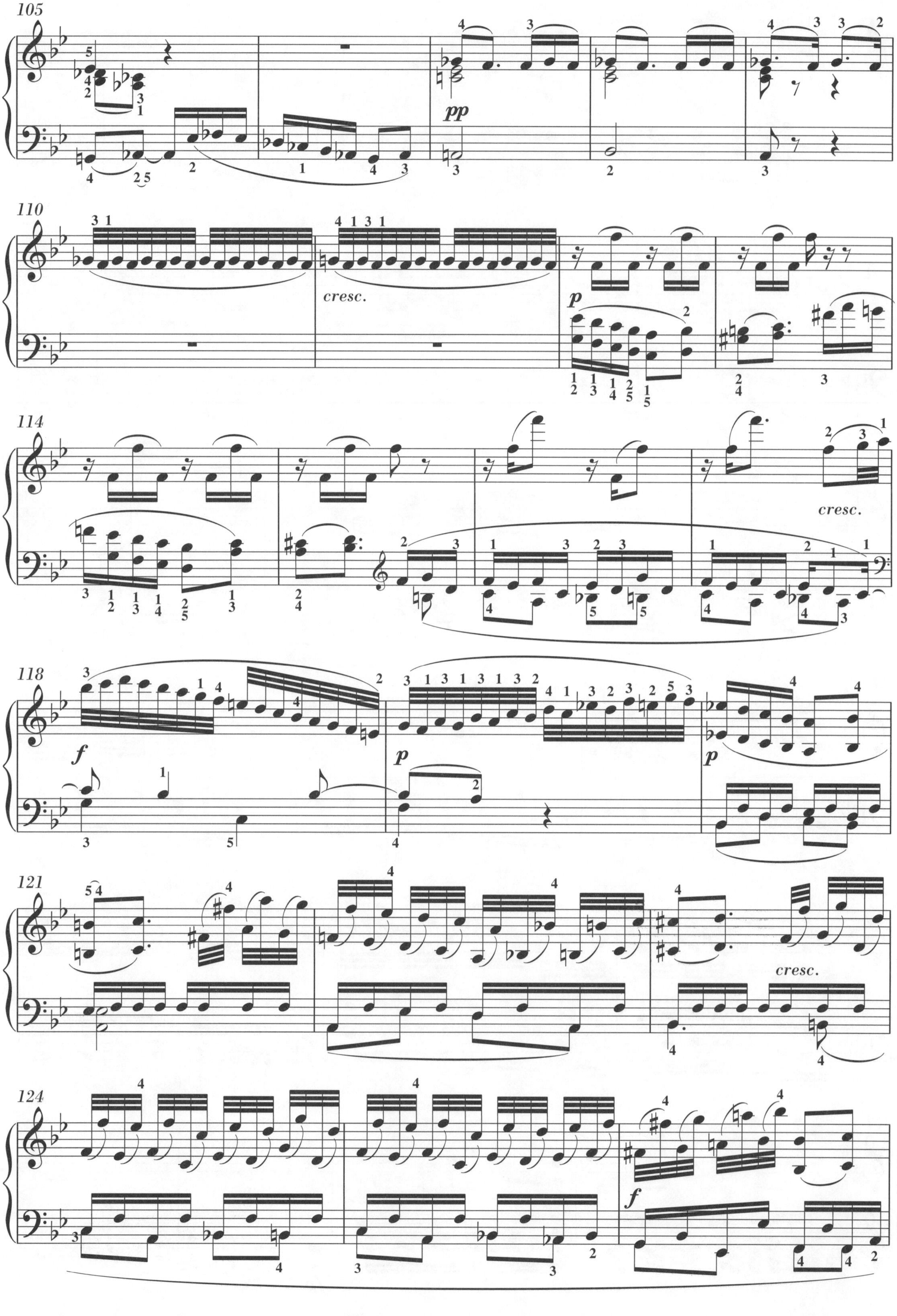
105
pp
110
cresc.
p
114
cresc.
118
f
p
p
121
cresc.
124
f

ABOUT THE EDITOR

ROBERT TAUB

From New York's Carnegie Hall to Hong Kong's Cultural Centre to Germany's *avant garde* Zentrum für Kunst und Medientechnologie, Robert Taub is acclaimed internationally. He has performed as soloist with the MET Orchestra in Carnegie Hall, the Boston Symphony Orchestra, BBC Philharmonic, The Philadelphia Orchestra, San Francisco Symphony, Los Angeles Philharmonic, Montreal Symphony, Munich Philharmonic, Orchestra of St. Luke's, Hong Kong Philharmonic, Singapore Symphony, and others.

Robert Taub has performed solo recitals on the Great Performers Series at New York's Lincoln Center and other major series worldwide. He has been featured in international festivals, including the Saratoga Festival, the Lichfield Festival in England, San Francisco's Midsummer Mozart Festival, the Geneva International Summer Festival, among others.

Following the conclusion of his highly celebrated New York series of Beethoven Piano Sonatas, Taub completed a sold-out Beethoven cycle in London at Hampton Court Palace. His recordings of the complete Beethoven Piano Sonatas have been praised throughout the world for their insight, freshness, and emotional involvement. In addition to performing, Robert Taub is an eloquent spokesman for music, giving frequent engaging and informal lectures and pre-concert talks. His book on Beethoven—*Playing the Beethoven Piano Sonatas*—has been published internationally by Amadeus Press.

Taub was featured in a recent PBS television program—*Big Ideas*—that highlighted him playing and discussing Beethoven Piano Sonatas. Filmed during his time as Artist-in-Residence at the Institute for Advanced Study, this program has been broadcast throughout the US on PBS affiliates.

Robert Taub's performances are frequently broadcast on radio networks around the world, including the NPR (Performance Today), Ireland's RTE, and Hong Kong's RTHK. He has also recorded the Sonatas of Scriabin and works of Beethoven, Schumann, Liszt, and Babbitt for Harmonia Mundi, several of which have been selected as "critic's favorites" by *Gramophone*, *Newsweek*, *The New York Times*, *The Washington Post*, *Ovation*, and *Fanfare*.

Robert Taub is involved with contemporary music as well as the established literature, premiering piano concertos by Milton Babbitt (MET Orchestra, James Levine) and Mel Powell (Los Angeles Philharmonic), and making the first recordings of the Persichetti Piano Concerto (Philadelphia Orchestra, Charles Dutoit) and Sessions Piano Concerto. He has premiered six works of Milton Babbitt (solo piano, chamber music, Second Piano Concerto). Taub has also collaborated with several 21st-century composers, including Jonathan Dawe (USA), David Bessell (UK), and Ludger Brümmer (Germany) performing their works in America and Europe.

Taub is a Phi Beta Kappa graduate of Princeton where he was a University Scholar. As a Danforth Fellow he completed his doctoral degree at The Juilliard School where he received the highest award in piano. Taub has served as Artist-in-Residence at Harvard University, at UC Davis, as well as at the Institute for Advanced Study. He has led music forums at Oxford and Cambridge Universities and The Juilliard School. Taub has also been Visiting Professor at Princeton University and at Kingston University (UK).